?*WHAT IF...*

SPACE

Steve Parker

Aladdin/Watts
London • Sydney

CONTENTS

© Aladdin Books Ltd 1995
Created and produced by
Aladdin Books Ltd
28 Percy Street
London W1P 0LD

*First published in Great Britain
in 1995 by*
Aladdin Books/Watts Books
96 Leonard Street
London EC2A 4RH
Designed by

David West • CHILDREN'S BOOKS
Designers
Rob Shone, Flick Killerby

Editor
Jon Richards

Illustrator
Peter Wilks – Simon Girling and
Associates

WHAT IF THERE WERE NO INTRODUCTION?

Well, you wouldn't be reading this! The *What If...?* books look at things from a very unusual angle, to make them exciting and interesting, as well as being packed with facts and fun.

The Universe is an unimaginably vast place. Our Earth is just a small part of the solar system, which, in turn, is a tiny speck within our galaxy, which is only one of millions of galaxies that whirl through space. Have you ever wondered what else might be out there? Well, *What If... Space?* describes how the Universe works, what's above our heads and how stars are born, live and die. It shows how planets, comets and asteroids orbit the Sun. It looks at how humanity sees the Universe, how we have taken our first steps into space and who might be out there, waiting for us. It does all this in a way that's easy to read and remember, by asking what might happen if... things were different!

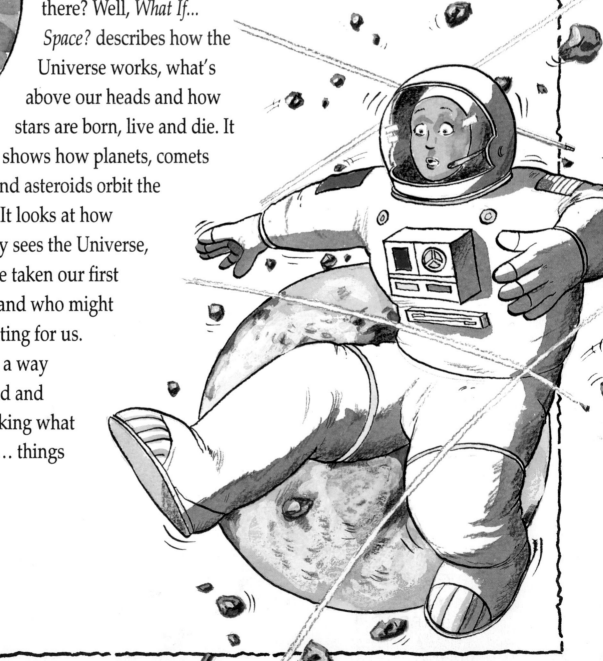

WHAT IF THE TELESCOPE HADN'T BEEN INVENTED?

We'd know very little about outer space, where stars, planets, moons, comets and other objects hurtle at incredible speeds across unimaginably vast distances. Our knowledge about space was given a great boost by the Italian scientist Galileo Galilei. In 1609 he turned a new-fangled telescope heavenwards and saw the Moon and planets magnified. It was a new era in astronomy, the study of space, stars and other heavenly objects. People have been star-gazing with telescopes ever since.

Geocentric or heliocentric?

In olden days, people believed in a geocentric system where the Sun and all the planets orbited around the Earth. However, astronomers such as Galileo found that their observations did not match this theory. They proposed a heliocentric system, where the Earth orbits the Sun. Today, we know this system is correct.

Galileo's improved telescope made objects look much larger. He saw that our Moon has mountains and craters, and that Jupiter has its own moons.

How could we see galaxies?

Even without a telescope, you can see a galaxy. The faint streak across the night sky is called the Milky Way, which is made up of millions of stars. It's actually our own galaxy. Telescopes reveal millions of other galaxies, or clusters of stars, in space.

Size isn't everything

The Universe is everything, including all of space, and every single star and other object. Without telescopes, we couldn't see very far across the Universe. With telescopes, we can detect incredibly distant objects. Scientists use these instruments to try and measure not just how large the Universe is, but also how long it's been around.

Why did an eclipse cause fear and terror?

Until people realised what happens during a solar eclipse (see page 11), these events caused panic and alarm. Many thought that angry gods were destroying the world, or that a massive dragon was trying to eat the Sun!

What if telescopes worked without light?

They do. Light rays are just one tiny part of a whole range of rays, called the electromagnetic spectrum. Stars send out light, and they also send out other rays in the spectrum, such as radio waves, X-rays and gamma rays. Radio telescopes with large dishes or long aerial wires and satellites detect the rays, to give us yet more information about space.

WHAT IF SPACE WEREN'T SPACE?

The space between stars, planets and other objects is not a complete vacuum (totally empty). There's a lot of emptiness, but there are rays and waves such as heat, light, radio waves and X-rays. There's also the odd molecule of hydrogen and other substances, sometimes forming huge clouds, called nebulae, that may be billions of kilometres across. There are also tiny particles, bits of dust and pieces of rock called micro-meteors, whizzing around. Near the Earth there's debris such as old rockets and satellites, space-station refuse, lost tools and other rubbish. They all make space-walks rather risky!

Earth
Mercury
Venus
Sun
Mars
Jupiter
Asteroid belt

Where is space crowded?

In the asteroid belt, between the planets Mars and Jupiter. Asteroids, also called minor planets, are big lumps of rock. They vary from about 500 km (312 miles) across to less than 100 m (333 ft). Millions of them make travelling through the asteroid belt very tricky!

What's a shooting star?

A famous movie actor with a gun? No, a shooting star is a lump of rock, called a meteor, that rushes through space and travels close to Earth. As it enters our atmosphere and pushes through the air, the friction, or rubbing against the air molecules, makes it hot. The meteor glows red-hot and burns up, creating a flash or trail of light. This is known as a shooting star (falling star). A large meteor might not burn up completely, and can smash onto the Earth's surface as a meteorite.

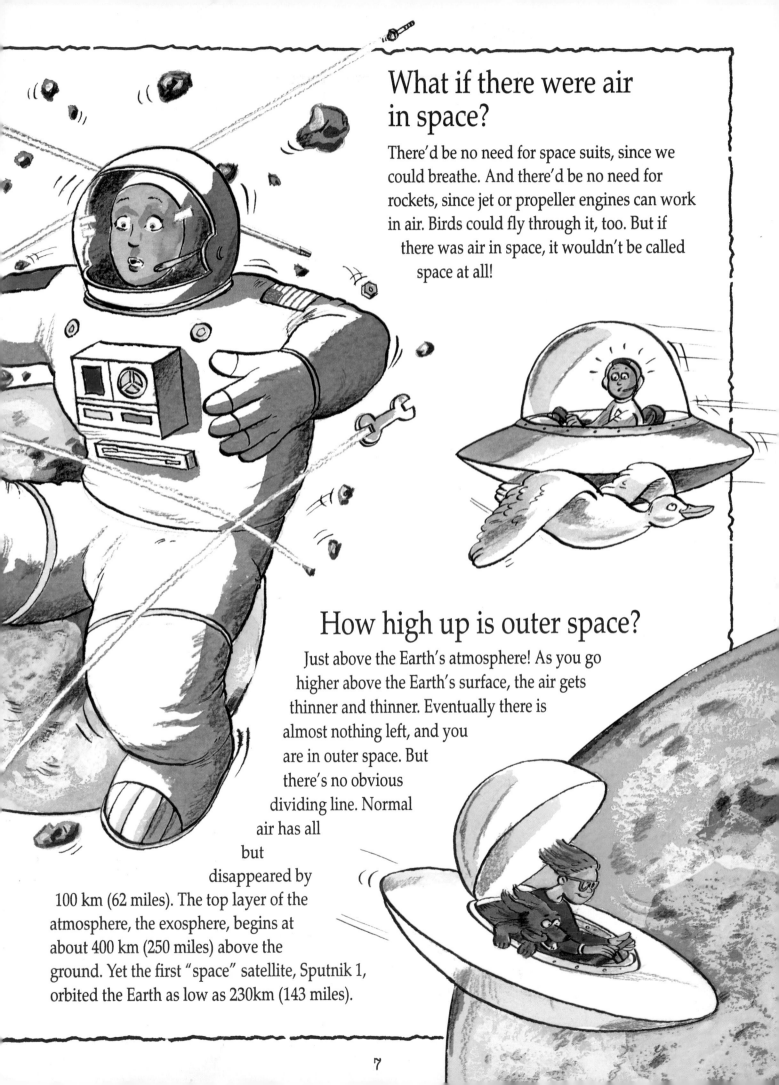

What if there were air in space?

There'd be no need for space suits, since we could breathe. And there'd be no need for rockets, since jet or propeller engines can work in air. Birds could fly through it, too. But if there was air in space, it wouldn't be called space at all!

How high up is outer space?

Just above the Earth's atmosphere! As you go higher above the Earth's surface, the air gets thinner and thinner. Eventually there is almost nothing left, and you are in outer space. But there's no obvious dividing line. Normal air has all but disappeared by 100 km (62 miles). The top layer of the atmosphere, the exosphere, begins at about 400 km (250 miles) above the ground. Yet the first "space" satellite, Sputnik 1, orbited the Earth as low as 230km (143 miles).

Could we land on Venus?

Venus is similar in size to Earth. But its atmosphere has clouds of corrosive sulphuric acid, and the surface temperature is 465°C (869°F). Not a place for a holiday!

Which planet is not named after a god?

All of them are named after Roman or Greek gods, except for Earth. It is named after the Old English word, "eorthe", meaning land or soil.

WHAT IF A SPACE PROBE TRIED TO LAND ON SATURN?

It would be very difficult, as there's hardly any "land" to land on! Saturn is the second largest planet, 120,536 km (75,335 miles) across, made mainly of the gases hydrogen and helium. A space probe would pass the planet's beautiful rings and disappear into the immense gas clouds of the atmosphere. As the probe fell deeper, the pressure would increase, and before long crush the probe. Further down, the pressure is so great that the gases are squeezed into liquid. The planet's core is a small, rocky lump.

The planet of fire and ice

Mercury, the planet closest to the Sun, is only 4,878 km (3,048 miles) across. Its atmosphere has been blasted away by powerful solar winds. The surface of this rocky ball experiences temperatures ranging from over 430°C (806°F – hot enough to melt lead), to a bone-chilling –180°C (–292°F)!

Stormy weather

Jupiter has a storm three times as big as the Earth, about 40,000 km (25,000 miles) across. It's called the Great Red Spot, and drifts around the planet's lower half. A gigantic vortex sucks up corrosive phosphorus and sulphur, in a huge swirling spiral. At the top of this spiral, the chemicals spill out, forming the huge spot, before falling back into the planet's atmosphere.

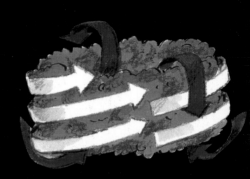

Are there canals on Mars?

Not really. But there are channels or canyons. In 1877 Italian astronomer Giovanni Schiaparelli described lines criss-crossing the surface of the "Red Planet". He called them canali which means "channels".

What are planetary rings made of?

Saturn has the biggest and best rings – six main ones, made up of hundreds of ringlets. They are 280,000 km (175,000 miles) in diameter – twice the planet's width. They are made from rocks, up to about 5 m (16 ft) across, swirling around the planet, and covered with ice. Jupiter, Neptune and Uranus also have fine rings.

Which planet is farthest from the Sun?

Pluto. No, Neptune. No – both! On average, Pluto is the outermost planet. This smallest, coldest world is only 2,300 km (1,438 miles) across, with a temperature of –220°C (–364°F). But its orbit is squashed, so for some of the time it's nearer to the Sun than its neighbour Neptune. In fact Pluto is within Neptune's orbit now, until 1999.

WHAT IF WE HAD LOADS OF MOONS?

If the Earth had lots of moons, our night creatures might get confused. Moths use the Moon to find their way around – which would they choose if there were more than one? Owls, bats and other night creatures might not wake up, as reflected light from the many moons would keep the night sky bright. The Earth would also be more like the other planets. Most have lots of moons going around them. At 3,476 km (2,160 miles) across, the Moon is very large compared to most moons of other planets. If we had lots of new moons, we'd have to invent new names for them.

Is there a man in the Moon?

No. There were men *on* the Moon – the US Apollo astronauts during 1969-72. The patterns that we see on the Moon's surface, looking like a crooked face, are made of giant mountains and massive craters. The craters, some up to 1,000 km (625 miles) across, were made when asteroids and meteorites smashed into the Moon's surface.

The birth of a moon

Some scientists believe the Moon was probably formed at the same time as the Earth, from rocks whirling in space. Others think it was made when a planet crashed into the Earth, throwing up masses of debris, which clumped together to form the Moon. The moons of other planets may have been asteroids captured by the planet's gravity.

Which planet has most moons?

At the moment Saturn has the most, with 18 moons as well as its colourful rings. This is followed by Jupiter with 16 and then Uranus which has 15. However, as telescopes get bigger and better, more moons may be discovered, so these numbers could change.

What happens if the Moon goes in front of the Sun?

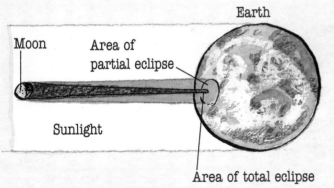

Earth

Moon   Area of partial eclipse

Sunlight

Area of total eclipse

It blots out the Sun and casts a shadow on the Earth, and we get a solar eclipse. But this does not happen all over the world. The total eclipse, with all the Sun hidden, is only in a small area. Around this is the area of partial eclipse, where the Sun appears to be only partly covered.

What's on the far side of the Moon?

The Moon goes around the Earth once every 27 days 8 hours. It also takes 27 days 8 hours to spin on its own axis. So the Moon always shows the same side to us. The far side of the Moon was first seen by the spacecraft Luna 3 in 1959, which sent back photographs of a lifeless moon, with no partying aliens!

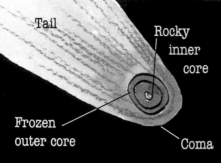

Tail

Rocky inner core

Frozen outer core

Coma

Inside a comet
A typical comet has a small centre, or core, a few kilometres across. It's made from bits of grit, dust and crystals of frozen gases such as methane, ammonia, carbon dioxide and water (ice).

WHAT IF COMETS DIDN'T RETURN?

Ancient people thought a comet was a god breathing into the heavens or sending a fireball to destroy Earth. At regular intervals they would streak across the night sky, creating fear and panic in all who saw them. However, comets are really just lumps of ice and rock that boil and fizz as they near the Sun, sending out an enormous tail of dust and vapour. In the 1700s astronomers noticed that these comets kept returning, orbiting the Sun in a stretched-out circle, called a parabola. But not all comets return. Some just disappear into space.

Crash, bang, wallop

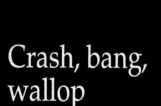

If a comet hit a planet, there would be a massive explosion. This was seen when the comet Shoemaker-Levy 9 collided with Jupiter in 1994. A series of explosions punched huge holes in the atmosphere, stirring up gases from Jupiter's interior.

How do we know comets will return?

The British astronomer Edmund Halley noticed that the paths of comets in 1531, 1607, and the one he saw in 1682, were all the same. Was it the same comet coming back? He predicted it would return in 1758. It did, and was named Halley's comet. Using his theories, astronomers were able to plot comets' long orbits around the Sun.

How do we know what's inside a comet?

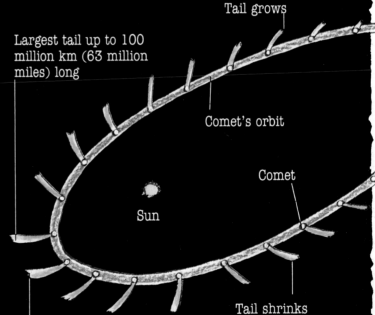

From observing its orbit and how fast it travels, studying the light and other waves it gives out and also using space probes. In 1986 five space probes passed near to Halley's comet, on its regular visit. Europe's Giotto got to within 600 km (375 miles) of the core, which is only 16 km (10 miles) long and 8 km (5 miles) wide, and sent back many photographs.

What if a comet didn't have a tail?

For much of its time, it doesn't. As a comet nears the Sun and warms, its icy crust boils, throwing out gases that make a glowing outer layer, the coma. The solar wind blows dust and other particles from the coma to form a tail that reflects the Sun's glow, and points away from the Sun. Then the comet heads into space, and the tail disappears.

Tail grows

Largest tail up to 100 million km (63 million miles) long

Comet's orbit

Comet

Sun

Tail shrinks

Tail points away from Sun

How long do comets last?

Some fall to bits after a few hundred years. Others may last millions of years. It depends partly on how often the comet comes near the Sun. Halley's comet has been seen every 75-76 years for over 2,000 years!

WHAT IF THE SUN WENT OUT?

Who turned off the lights? Why is it suddenly so cold? If the Sun no longer bathed our world in light and warmth, we might last a short time, with fires and electric light and heat. But plants could not grow in the dark, and animals would perish from cold. Soon all life would cease, and our planet would be dark, dead and frozen. In fact this will happen! Our Sun is a fairly typical star, and stars do not last for ever. They form, grow old, and either fade away or explode in a supernova, a massive explosion. But don't worry, this won't happen to the Sun for billions of years yet!

From the cradle to the grave

Throughout the Universe there are massive clouds of gas, called nebulae. In some of these, the dust and particles are clumping together, and over millions of years, these clumps will form stars. Other nebulae are the wispy remains of a supernova, a star that has exploded. So these are star graveyards.

What is a red giant?

An enormous human with red clothes? No, it is a star that has been growing and shining for billions of years, and is nearing the end of its life. As it ages, the star swells and its light turns red. Our Sun will do this in billions of years. It will expand to the size of a Red Giant, scorching our planet, before it explodes. Then all that will be left is a tiny white dwarf star that will slowly fade over millions of years.

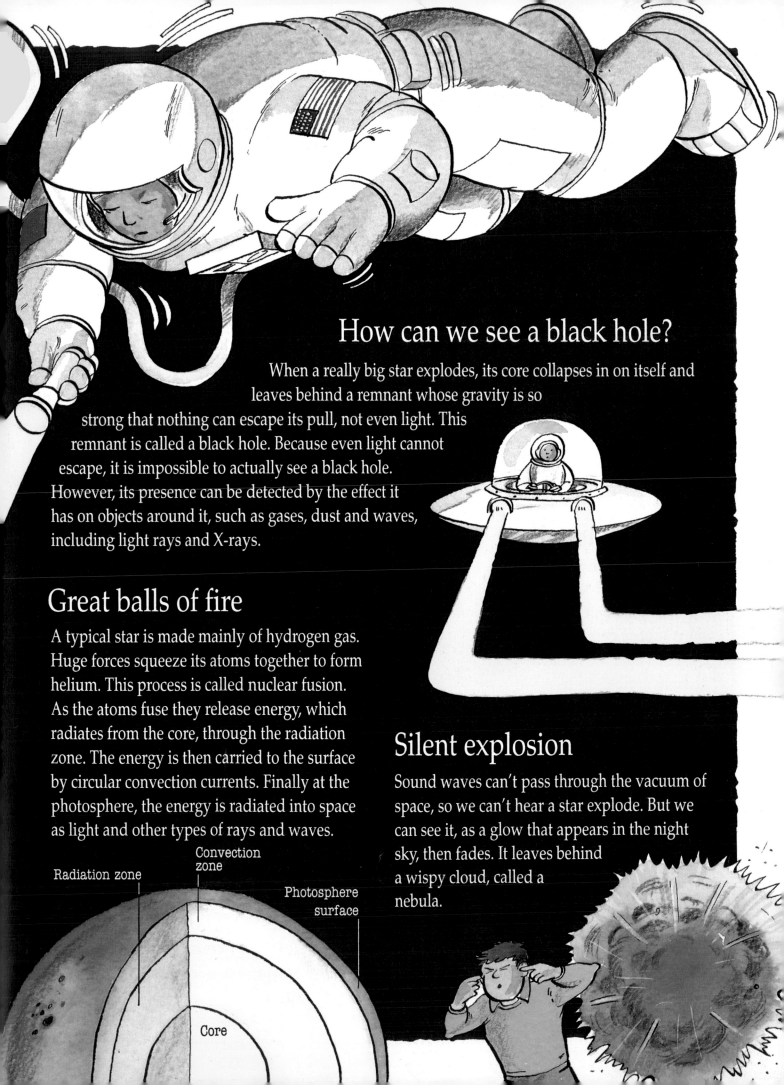

How can we see a black hole?

When a really big star explodes, its core collapses in on itself and leaves behind a remnant whose gravity is so strong that nothing can escape its pull, not even light. This remnant is called a black hole. Because even light cannot escape, it is impossible to actually see a black hole. However, its presence can be detected by the effect it has on objects around it, such as gases, dust and waves, including light rays and X-rays.

Great balls of fire

A typical star is made mainly of hydrogen gas. Huge forces squeeze its atoms together to form helium. This process is called nuclear fusion. As the atoms fuse they release energy, which radiates from the core, through the radiation zone. The energy is then carried to the surface by circular convection currents. Finally at the photosphere, the energy is radiated into space as light and other types of rays and waves.

Radiation zone

Convection zone

Photosphere surface

Core

Silent explosion

Sound waves can't pass through the vacuum of space, so we can't hear a star explode. But we can see it, as a glow that appears in the night sky, then fades. It leaves behind a wispy cloud, called a nebula.

Dizzy galaxies

A galaxy is a group of billions of stars. Our own galaxy is called a spiral. It has long, curved arms, and it spins like a catherine-wheel firework. Other galaxies are ellipticals (oval) or irregulars (no shape).

How did ancient people view the Universe?

Many ancient cultures were fascinated by the stars. According to some theories, the Ancient Egyptians tried to construct a replica of the heavens around the Nile, which represented the Milky Way. The three great pyramids represented Orion's belt.

WHAT IF THERE WERE NO STARS AT NIGHT?

Sometimes there aren't, if it's cloudy. Well, the stars are still there, but we can't see them. Without stars, the Ancient Greeks and others wouldn't have spent hours gazing at them. They would not have imagined the outlines of people and objects in the star patterns. So we would not have constellations, such as Orion (the Hunter) and Centaur (half man, half horse). Also, navigators couldn't use star charts to find their way across seas. So explorers might never have discovered the Americas, Australia and the Pacific islands.

Zoo in the sky

The stars in the night sky are divided into patterns and groups, known as constellations (see above). These were named after people from legends and even animals. The northern hemisphere has two bears, the great bear (Ursa major) and the little bear (Ursa minor). Find some star charts and try to look for the constellations tonight. The night sky also has a bird of paradise (Apus), a ram (Aries), a toucan (Tucana), a wolf (Lupus), a whale (Cetus), a fox (Vulpecula), a dolphin (Delphinus) and a snake (Serpens). All they need now is a zoo keeper!

What if the stars moved?

They do. Stars in our spiral galaxy are spinning around. Our Sun takes over 200 million years to orbit the centre of the galaxy. As the stars move, star patterns and constellations gradually change. In thousands of years, constellations will be different, and today's star charts will be out of date and useless.

What if the planets shone, like stars?

It would probably never get dark! Planets shine, but only because they reflect the light from the Sun. However, they are not massive enough to start the process of nuclear fusion which makes stars shine (see page 15).

WHAT IF THE UNIVERSE STARTED TO SHRINK?

Echoes in space

Radio telescopes picking up microwaves detect a background "hiss" in space. It shows the temperature of the Universe is slightly warmer in some parts than others. These "ripples" are echoes of the Big Bang.

Most experts believe that the Universe began as a tiny speck containing all matter, which blew up billions of years ago in a massive explosion, called the Big Bang. It's been getting bigger ever since, as galaxies fly away from one another. This may go on for ever, or the Universe might reach a certain size, and maintain what is called a steady state, or it could begin to shrink. All the planets, stars, galaxies and other matter might squeeze back together into a tiny speck as the opposite of the Big Bang – the Big Crunch.

What was the Big Bang?

It was the beginning of the Universe: the time when all matter began to explode and expand, from a small centre full of incredible heat, light and energy. Was there anything before the Big Bang, like a supreme being? No one knows. There may have been no "before". Space, and matter, and energy, and even time, may have started with the Big Bang.

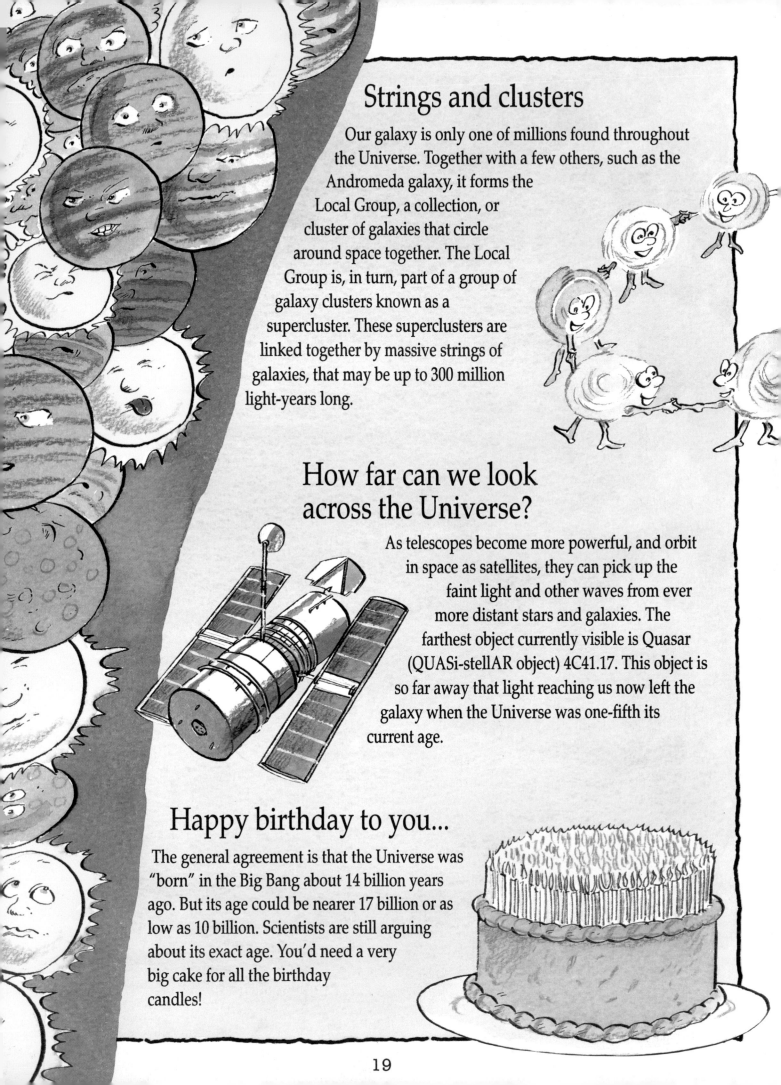

Strings and clusters

Our galaxy is only one of millions found throughout the Universe. Together with a few others, such as the Andromeda galaxy, it forms the Local Group, a collection, or cluster of galaxies that circle around space together. The Local Group is, in turn, part of a group of galaxy clusters known as a supercluster. These superclusters are linked together by massive strings of galaxies, that may be up to 300 million light-years long.

How far can we look across the Universe?

As telescopes become more powerful, and orbit in space as satellites, they can pick up the faint light and other waves from ever more distant stars and galaxies. The farthest object currently visible is Quasar (QUASi-stellAR object) 4C41.17. This object is so far away that light reaching us now left the galaxy when the Universe was one-fifth its current age.

Happy birthday to you...

The general agreement is that the Universe was "born" in the Big Bang about 14 billion years ago. But its age could be nearer 17 billion or as low as 10 billion. Scientists are still arguing about its exact age. You'd need a very big cake for all the birthday candles!

WHAT IF THERE WERE NO SPACECRAFT?

Space exploration would be much less exciting without spacecraft to carry people. It began with the Space Race in the 1950s and 1960s. The United States and Russia raced to launch the first satellite, the first spaceman and woman, and the first Moon visit. The satellite Sputnik 1, launched in 1957, was the first man-made object in space, and the Russian Yuri Gagarin was the first man in space. But Neil Armstrong of the United States was first to land on the Moon, in 1969. Without spacecraft, none of these would have happened, and any future discoveries, including finding aliens, would have a long time to wait.

How would astronauts get back to Earth?

An astronaut could survive in a space suit for a short time. But coming back into Earth's atmosphere creates lots of heat, as an object pushes through the ever-thickening air molecules. A heat shield might help a rear-first re-entry!

What would Yuri Gagarin have done?

Yuri was the very first person in space. On 12 April, 1961 he orbited Earth once in his ball-shaped spacecraft Vostok 1. Without this spacecraft, he would never have become world famous. But he could have carried on as a test pilot for the Russian Air Force.

What if there were no satellites?

We'd have no satellite TV or satellite weather pictures. Mobile phones would not work so well. Ships, planes and overland explorers could not use their satellite navigation gadgets. Without satellites, countries would have to find new ways to spy on each other. They could go back to the high-flying spy planes used just after World War Two, or use high-flying balloons carrying surveillance equipment.

How much money would we save?

Space programmes run throughout the world by different countries, like the Apollo Moon missions, have cost billions of dollars. Manned space flights are the most expensive type of mission. It has been estimated that NASA has spent over $80 billion on its manned space flights up to 1994, with nearly $45 billion spent on the space shuttle programme alone! Even a single space suit worn outside the space shuttle costs $3.4 million!

Frying pans and microchips

Our everyday lives have been affected by the enormous technological leaps made during the age of space exploration. These "leaps" include non-stick coatings, used for lubrication in spacecraft, and now found on frying pans. Also, the micro-technology needed in satellites has led to smaller and faster computers, some found in household appliances.

WELCOME EARTHLINGS!

WHAT IF ROCKETS HADN'T BEEN INVENTED?

We'd still be wondering about the empty sky above us, instead of launching astronauts into space and sending probes on space missions. A rocket engine can fly fast enough to reach space. To do this, it must reach escape velocity, 28,500 km/h (17,700 mph), when it can break free from the pull of Earth's gravity. Also a rocket engine can work in airless space, unlike jets and other engines, as explained below. The only other way to get into space might be a gigantic gun that fires spacecraft and satellites into space. However, any astronaut would be crushed by the g-forces of acceleration!

Dawn of the rocket age

The first rockets were used by the Chinese over 1,000 years ago and were fuelled by a type of gunpowder. The first rocket to use liquid fuel was launched by American scientist Robert Goddard in 1926.

Why can't jets fly in space?

Like a jet engine, a rocket burns fuel in a type of continuous explosion. Hot gases blast out of the back, and thrust the engine forward. However, space has no oxygen, which is needed for the burning that takes place inside the jet engine. A rocket must carry its own oxygen.

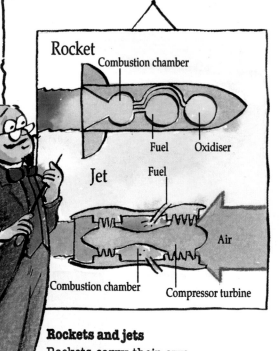

Rockets and jets
Rockets carry their own oxidiser substance. Jets, however, need oxygen from the air to burn their fuel.

Up, up and away in my beautiful balloon

Special weather balloons go higher than 50 km (31 miles). They carry radiosondes, which are instruments that measure temperature, air pressure and humidity, and send back the results by radio. The balloons are quite small and floppy when they take off, but they expand as they rise, as the air pressure gets less. However, no balloon could carry a heavy satellite high enough, or give it enough forward speed to put the satellite in orbit.

Would we have fantastically fabulous firework displays?

Perhaps, but we'd have to power the rockets by other types of engines, maybe a mini jet engine. Firework rockets use solid fuel, such as gunpowder or other powdery fuel-oxidiser mixtures to launch into the air. Many space rockets use liquid fuel, and have the propellant and oxidiser in liquid form.

Multi-staged rockets

A staged rocket may have two, three or more rockets, placed on top of each other in decreasing size. The biggest one launches the entire rocket, then stops firing and falls away. The rocket's weight is now less and so is the effect of the Earth's gravity, so the second-stage rocket is much smaller. This continues with the remaining stages. Extra rockets, known as boosters, may assist the main rocket engine at launch and then fall away, as in the space shuttle. These parachute into the sea, to be recovered and used again.

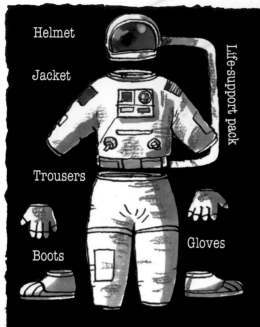

Helmet

Jacket

Trousers

Boots

Gloves

Life-support pack

Sections of a space suit
The suit has various parts, and it takes a long time to put on. All the joins must be airtight, to maintain proper air pressure and temperature.

WHAT IF THE SPACE SUIT HADN'T BEEN INVENTED?

Astronauts are safe in space, if they stay inside their spacecraft. Outside, there is no air to breathe. It is also incredibly cold (or hot) and there are lots of dangerous rays and radiation. The space suit is shiny to reflect rays of radiation, and it contains its own life-support systems that control the air and temperature. It also has special layers to protect against impact from debris, such as micro-meteors which travel as fast as tiny bullets. In space, any other type of suit, like a deep-sea diver's suit, would be no good at all!

How could we repair satellites?

If a satellite malfunctions, astronauts can manoeuvre their spacecraft near it, then float over in a space suit with a jet-pack, to make repairs. If space suits didn't exist we might have to invent a robot repair man!

Would Alexei Leonov be so famous?

This Russian spaceman became famous on 18 March 1965. He was first to use a space suit to leave his craft for a space "walk", floating weightlessly, miles above the Earth.

Could people have landed on the Moon?

Yes, but they couldn't have walked around. The Moon has no atmosphere, so the astronauts would have had to stay in their spacecraft.

Leaky space suits

The suit contains a mixture of gases for breathing. It's under pressure, to simulate the Earth's atmosphere. If it squirts away through a leak, the astronaut will be in great danger!

What if space suits weren't cooled?

Or warmed, either? In Earth's orbit, the astronaut orbits the planet in about 90 minutes. He would get boiling hot while in the glare of the Sun. As he circled around to the night side, he'd freeze to death! The space suit keeps his body temperature within a more comfortable range.

WHAT IF WE COULD TRAVEL AT THE SPEED OF LIGHT?

Almost everything in the Universe varies from place to place, such as temperature, gravity, and the size and mass of objects. However, the speed of light is always the same – 299,792 kilometres per second (186,282 miles per second). As you approach the speed of light, strange things happen, according to Albert Einstein's theory of relativity.

What is a light-year?

365 sunny days? No, it is not a measure of time, but of distance. It's the distance that light travels in one year. Since light travels very fast, a light-year is extremely far, about 9.46 trillion km (5.88 trillion miles) Even so, space is so vast that a light-year is a tiny distance.

Time slows down relative to the outside world and objects get smaller and heavier. Modern science says that no physical matter could travel faster than light, or even at the speed of light. However, waves and rays, such as radio waves and X-rays, travel as fast as light, since they are part of the same electromagnetic spectrum (see page 5).

Space, the final frontier...

In science fiction stories, such as *Star Trek*, characters are always travelling from solar system to solar system in search of adventure. However, even if we could travel at the speed of light, it would still take over four years to reach Proxima Centauri, our nearest star after the Sun. Even then, we would have to find a planet to land on.

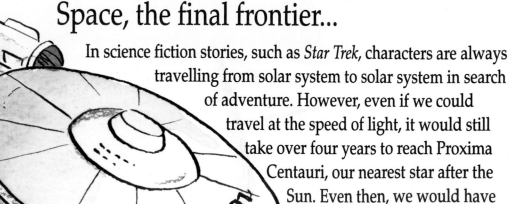

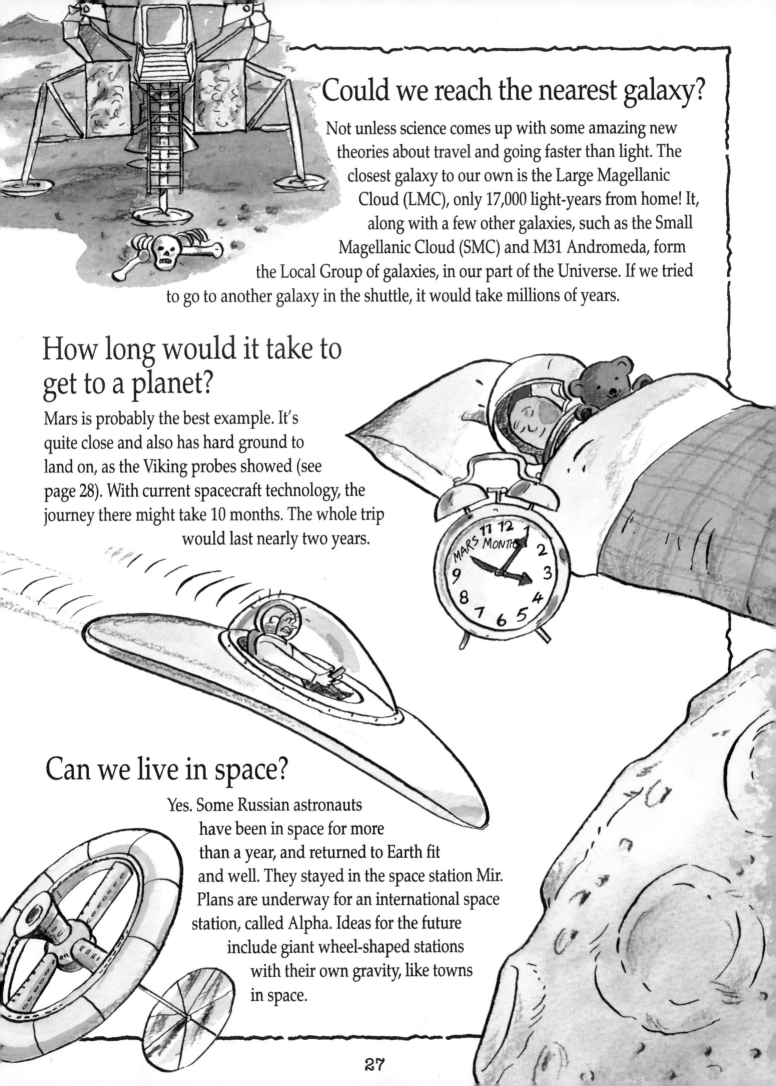

Could we reach the nearest galaxy?

Not unless science comes up with some amazing new theories about travel and going faster than light. The closest galaxy to our own is the Large Magellanic Cloud (LMC), only 17,000 light-years from home! It, along with a few other galaxies, such as the Small Magellanic Cloud (SMC) and M31 Andromeda, form the Local Group of galaxies, in our part of the Universe. If we tried to go to another galaxy in the shuttle, it would take millions of years.

How long would it take to get to a planet?

Mars is probably the best example. It's quite close and also has hard ground to land on, as the Viking probes showed (see page 28). With current spacecraft technology, the journey there might take 10 months. The whole trip would last nearly two years.

Can we live in space?

Yes. Some Russian astronauts have been in space for more than a year, and returned to Earth fit and well. They stayed in the space station Mir. Plans are underway for an international space station, called Alpha. Ideas for the future include giant wheel-shaped stations with their own gravity, like towns in space.

WHAT IF THERE WERE MARTIANS?

Are UFOs real?

Unidentified Flying Objects certainly exist. People, including jet-plane pilots, see things in the sky they cannot identify. But are they alien spacecraft? They could be test planes, meteors, or even the planet Venus!

The space probes, Vikings 1 and 2, landed on Mars in 1976. They found a reddish, dusty, rock-strewn landscape. But their cameras, sensors and experiments detected no proper sign of life. In August 1993, as the space probe Mars Observer approached its destination, its radio failed, and all went silent. Was it sabotaged by shy, secretive Martians? Probably not. Scientists estimate that among 10 billion galaxies, there are trillions of stars, and probably some that have planets like Earth – maybe these have some kind of life.

Are we trying to send messages to aliens?

Yes, we send bursts of radio messages into space. Also, space probes carry messages in case they are found by aliens. Pioneers 10 and 11 have plaques with a star map showing where we are, and drawings of humans.

Are aliens trying to get in touch with us?

Perhaps, but messages in bottles or shouting won't work! Only light, radio and similar waves travel through space at great speed. Clever aliens might send messages as coded patterns of waves. Radio telescopes of the SETI (Search for Extra-Terrestrial Intelligence) project try to detect such waves, but have had no luck so far.

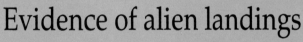

What if they landed?

There's a plan for dealing with aliens. But it's secret. Anyway, aliens advanced enough for space travel would be much smarter than we are. So it wouldn't matter what we did. We just hope they are friendly!

Evidence of alien landings

A few strange cave drawings, paintings, sculptures and rock patterns from ancient times, might suggest that aliens visited Earth long ago. Some people say that over the years, aliens have helped us. But there's no real proof, and that's what scientists require.

FACTFILE

PLANET PROFILES

Planetary year is time taken to
make one orbit of the Sun
Planetary day is time taken to
spin once on axis

MERCURY
Diameter: 4,878 km (3,031 miles)
Average distance from Sun:
  58 million km (36 million miles)
Planetary year: 88 Earth days
Planetary day: 59 Earth days
Surface temperature range:
  –183 to 430°C (–292 to 806 °F)

VENUS
Diameter: 12,105 km (7,520 miles)
Average distance from Sun:
  108 million km (67 million miles)
Planetary year: 225 Earth days
Planetary day: 243 Earth days
Surface temperature:
  av. 465°C (869°F)

EARTH
Diameter: 12,756 km (7,926 miles)
Average distance from Sun:
  150 million km (93 million miles)
Planetary year: 365 days
Planetary day: 24 hours
Surface temperature:
  av. 15°C (59°F)

MARS
Diameter: 6,786 km (4,217 miles)
Average distance from Sun:
  228 million km (142 million miles)
Planetary year: 687 Earth days
Planetary day: 24.6 Earth hours
Surface temperature range:
  –133 to 22°C (–207 to 72°F)

JUPITER
Diameter: 142,984 km
  (88,846 miles)
Average distance from Sun:
  778 million km
  (483 million miles)
Planetary year: 11.8 Earth years
Planetary day: 9.9 Earth hours
Surface temperature:
  av. –150°C (–238°F)

SATURN
Diameter: 120,536 km
  (74,898 miles)
Average distance from Sun:
  1,427 million km
  (887 million miles)
Planetary year: 29.5 Earth years
Planetary day: 10.5 Earth hours
Surface temperature:
  av. –180°C (–292°F)

URANUS
Diameter: 51,118 km (31,763 miles)
Average distance from Sun:
  2,871 million km
  (1,784 million miles)
Planetary year: 84 Earth years
Planetary day: 17.25 Earth hours
Surface temperature:
  av. –210°C (–346°F)

NEPTUNE
Diameter: 49,528 km (30,775 miles)
Average distance from Sun:
  4,497 million km
  (2,794 million miles)
Planetary year: 164.8 Earth years
Planetary day: 16 Earth hours
Surface temperature:
  av. –210°C (–346°F)

PLUTO
Diameter: 2,280 km (1,419 miles)
Average distance from Sun:
  5,900 million km
  (3,688 million miles)
Planetary year: 247.7 Earth years
Planetary day: 6.4 Earth days
Surface temperature:
  av. –220°C (–364°F)

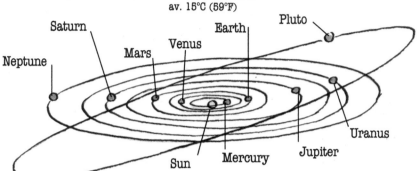

The Solar System

Jupiter

Saturn

GLOSSARY

FROM BIG TO SMALL

Universe Everything, including all galaxies, stars, planets and other objects, as well as space, cosmic dust and all other matter between them.

Galaxy A huge group or cluster of stars relatively close together, separated by vast, empty space from other galaxies. Our own galaxy is called The Galaxy or Milky Way.

Quasar (Quasi-stellar object) A mysterious and extremely distant object that shines like many galaxies, but which seems smaller in size than one galaxy. It may be a galaxy being born.

Solar system A collection of planets that orbit a star. Our solar system has a total of nine planets that go round the Sun.

Star In astronomy, a star is an object that gives out energy as light, heat and other forms of radiation. In other words, it shines under its own power.

Sun Our local star, which seems so bright and warm because it's relatively close to us. The Sun is quite small as stars go, and is termed a yellow dwarf.

White dwarf A small type or stage in the life of a star, possibly not much bigger than a planet such as Jupiter. It is usually a star that is reaching the end of its life.

Planet A relatively large object that goes around a star, such as the nine planets orbiting the Sun.

Moon An object in space that orbits (goes around) a larger object, usually a planet. Earth has one large moon, which we call the Moon. Moons are also satellites.

Asteroid A small, rocky body that is also known as a minor planet. In our solar system the greatest concentration of asteroids is in the asteroid belt between the planets Mars and Jupiter.

Satellite An object in space that orbits (goes around) a larger object. So Earth is a satellite of the Sun, and the Moon is a satellite of the Earth. But the word "satellite" is usually used to mean an artificial or man-made space object.

Black hole A region in space that has incredible gravity, so nothing can escape from it, not even light or other forms of energy. Any nearby matter is pulled into it.

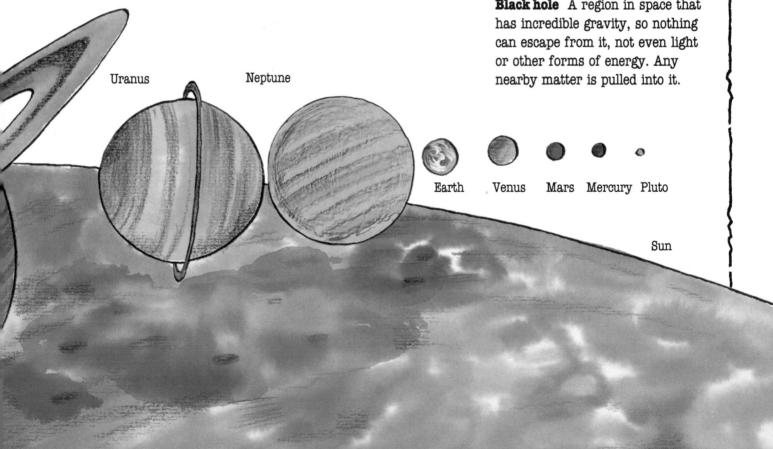

Uranus Neptune Earth Venus Mars Mercury Pluto Sun

INDEX

PRINTED IN BELGIUM BY
proost
INTERNATIONAL BOOK PRODUCTION